of co-ordination
is both valuable and
important to a child's later
development, and this is found,
for instance, in *Finger Rhymes*,
the first book of the eight book series.

This series provides an enjoyable introduction to poetry, music and dance for every young child. Most books of this type have only a few rhymes for each age group, whereas each book of this series is intended for a particular age group. There is a strong tcaching sequence in the selection of rhymes, from the first simple ways of winning the child's interest by toe tapping and palm tickling jingles, through practice in numbers, memory and pronunciation, to combining sound, action and words. For the first time young children can learn rhymes in a sequence that is related to their age.

## Contents

*LEARNING WITH TRADITIONAL RHYMES*

# Action Rhymes

by DOROTHY TAYLOR
with illustrations by
KATHY LAYFIELD & BRIAN PRICE THOMAS
and photographs by JOHN MOYES

Ladybird Books Loughborough

## *One finger, one thumb keep moving*

One finger, one thumb keep moving,
One finger, one thumb keep moving,
One finger, one thumb keep moving,
We'll all be merry and bright.

One finger, one thumb, one arm, keep moving,
One finger, one thumb, one arm, keep moving,
One finger, one thumb, one arm, keep moving,
We'll all be merry and bright.

One finger, one thumb, one arm, *one leg*,
keep moving, etc.

One finger, one thumb, one arm, one leg,
*one nod of the head*, keep moving, etc.

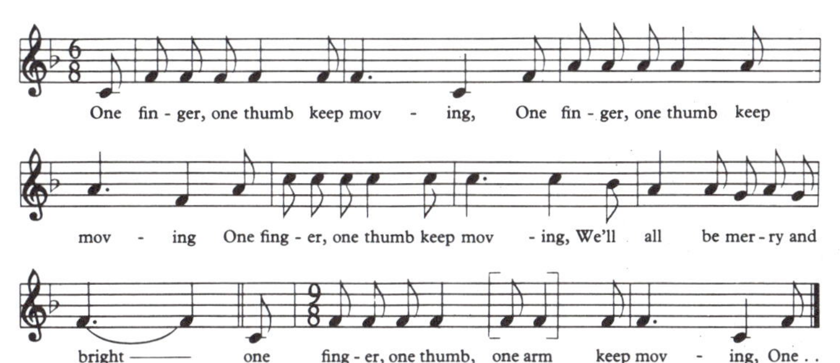
One fin - ger, one thumb keep mov - ing, One fin - ger, one thumb keep
mov - ing One fing - er, one thumb keep mov - ing, We'll all be mer - ry and
bright —— one fing - er, one thumb, one arm keep mov - ing, One . .

# *Cobbler, cobbler, mend my shoe*

Cobbler, cobbler, mend my shoe,
*Hammer on knees with fists.*

Get it done by half past two.

My toe is peeping through,
*Drum feet on floor.*

Cobbler, cobbler, mend my shoe.
*Hammer on knees with fists.*

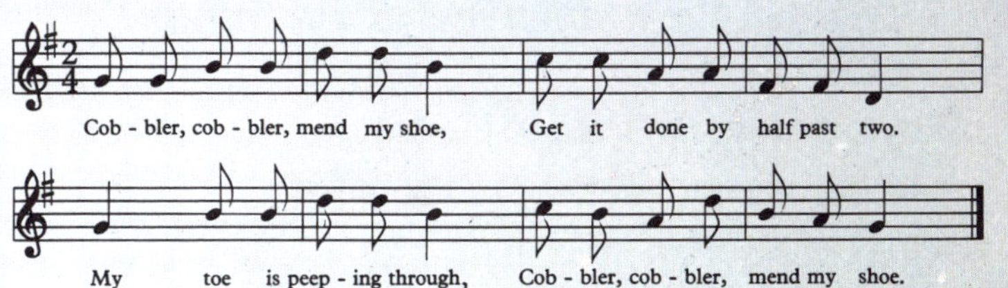
Cob - bler, cob - bler, mend my shoe, Get it done by half past two.
My toe is peep - ing through, Cob - bler, cob - bler, mend my shoe.

## *There was a man lived in the moon*

There was a man lived in the moon,
Lived in the moon, lived in the moon,
There was a man lived in the moon,
And his name was Aiken Drum.

*And he played upon a ladle,*
*A ladle, a ladle,*
*And he played upon a ladle,*
*And his name was Aiken Drum.*

And his hat was made of good cream cheese,
Of good cream cheese, of good cream cheese,
And his hat was made of good cream cheese,
And his name was Aiken Drum.

*And he played upon a ladle, etc.*

And his coat was made of good roast beef, etc.

And his buttons were made of penny loaves, etc.

And his waistcoat was made of crust of pies, etc.

And his breeches were made of haggis bags, etc.

*The children can mime each verse of this rhyme—Verse 1, point to sky (for moon), Verse 2, touch head (for hat), Verse 3, clutch collar (for coat), and so on, strumming as with guitar during chorus.*

There was a man lived in the moon

## *Row, row, row your boat*

Row, row, row your boat,
Gently down the stream.
Merrily, merrily, merrily, merrily,
Life is but a dream.

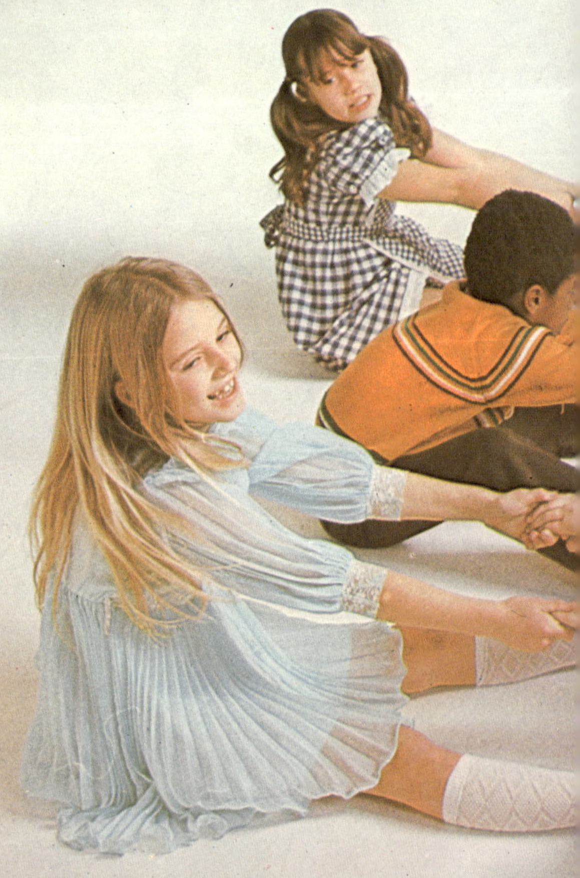

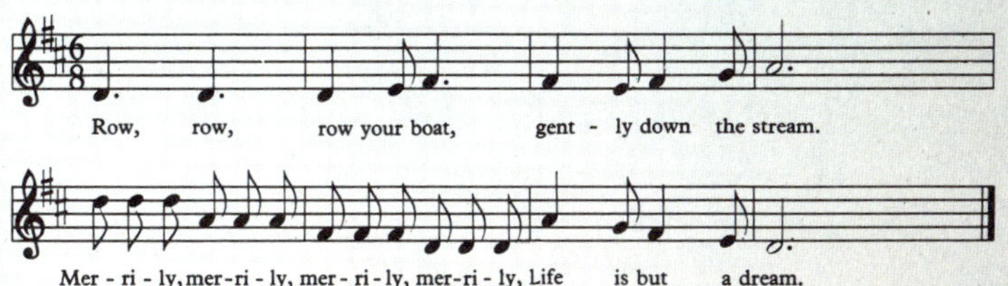
Row, row, row your boat, gent - ly down the stream.
Mer - ri - ly, mer-ri - ly, mer - ri - ly, mer-ri - ly, Life is but a dream.

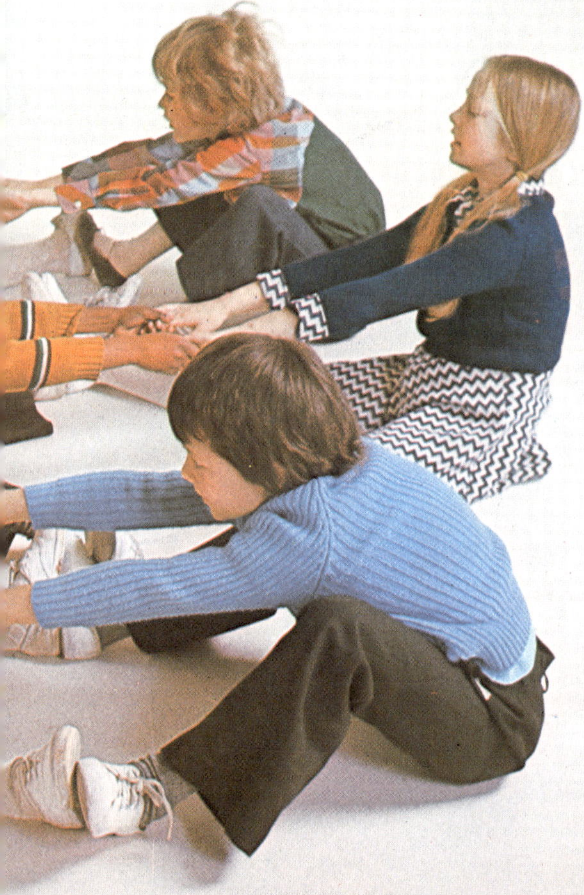

## *Can you plant your cabbages*

Can you plant your cabbages
In the right way, in the right way?
Can you plant your cabbages
In the right way, just like us?

You can plant them with your foot,
In the right way, in the right way.
You can plant them with your foot
In the right way, just like us.

You can plant them with your hand,
In the right way, in the right way.
You can plant them with your hand
In the right way, just like us.

*The children tap with their feet and pat with their hands on the appropriate words.*

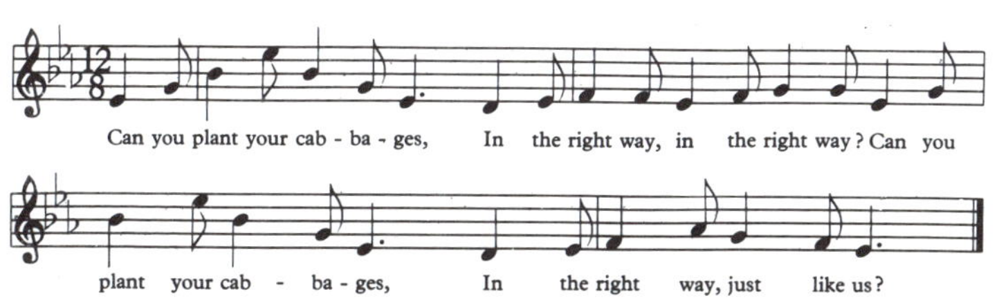

## *Are you sleeping, are you sleeping*

Are you sleeping, are you sleeping,
Brother John, Brother John?
Ring the bells for matins,
Ring the bells for matins,
Ding, ding, dong.
Ding, ding, dong.

# *Frère Jacques, Frère Jacques*

Frère Jacques, Frère Jacques,
Dormez-vous, dormez-vous?
Sonnez les matines, sonnez les matines,
Din, din, don.
Din, din, don.

*The most usual miming action performed to this rhyme is bell-pulling.*

## *Oh, we can play on the big bass drum*

Oh, we can play on the big bass drum,
And this is the way we do it:
Boom, boom, boom, goes the big bass drum,
And that's the way we do it.

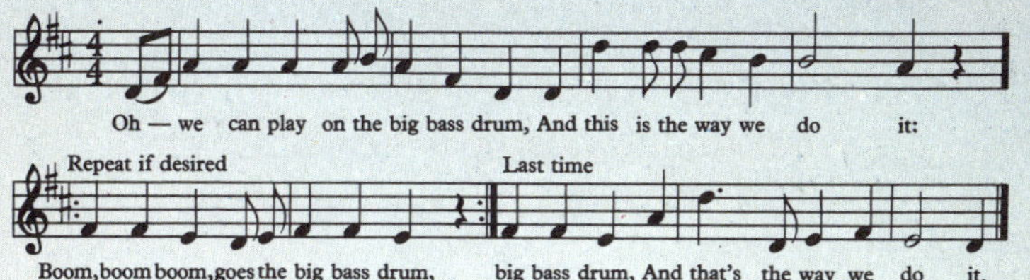


*In this rhyme, each child is asked to mime an instrument, following the words.*

Oh, we can play on the violin,
And this is the way we do it:
Fiddle-diddle-dee, goes the violin,
And that's the way we do it.

*Flute . . . tootle-toot-toot*

*Double-bass . . . zum, zum, zum*

*Tambourine . . . chink, chink, chink*

*Triangle . . . ting, ting, ting*

*Castanet . . . clacka, clacka, clack*

# *Old McDonald had a farm*

Old McDonald had a farm
E . . . I . . . E . . . I . . . O
And on that farm he had some cows,
E . . . I . . . E . . . I . . . O
With a moo-moo here,
And a moo-moo there,
Here a moo, there a moo,
Everywhere a moo-moo,
Old McDonald had a farm,
E . . . I . . . E . . . I . . . O

Old McDonald had a farm,
E . . . I . . . E . . . I . . . O
And on that farm he had some ducks,
E . . . I . . . E . . . I . . . O
With a quack-quack here, . . . etc.

. . . *cats* . . . mew-mew . . .

. . . *horses* . . . neigh-neigh . . .

. . . *dogs* . . . woof-woof . . .

. . . *lambs* . . . baa-baa . . .

*Adjust the speed of this song to suit the age of the child; older children can be encouraged to memorise what has gone before*

*e.g. 'with a quack-quack here,*
*And a quack-quack there,*
*Here a quack, there a quack,*
*Everywhere a quack-quack,*
*Moo-moo-here, moo-moo-there, etc.*

*Old McDonald had a farm*

## *Peter hammers with one hammer*

Peter hammers with one hammer,
*Bang on the floor with one foot.*
One hammer, one hammer,
Peter hammers with one hammer,
All day long.

Peter hammers with two hammers,

*Two fists.*

Two hammers, two hammers,
Peter hammers with two hammers,
All day long.

Peter hammers with *three* hammers, etc.

*Fists and one foot.*

Peter hammers with *four* hammers, etc.

*Fists and both feet.*

Peter hammers with *five* hammers, etc.

*Fists, feet, nodding head.*

## *Sing a song of sixpence*

Sing a song of sixpence,
A pocket full of rye;
Four and twenty blackbirds
Baked in a pie!
When the pie was opened
The birds began to sing;
Wasn't that a dainty dish
To set before the king?

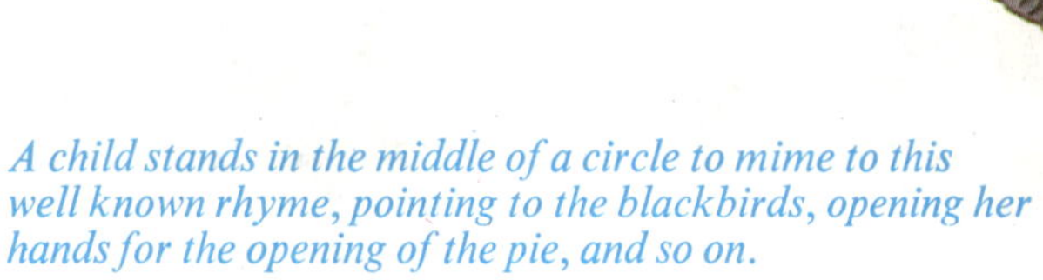

*A child stands in the middle of a circle to mime to this well known rhyme, pointing to the blackbirds, opening her hands for the opening of the pie, and so on.*

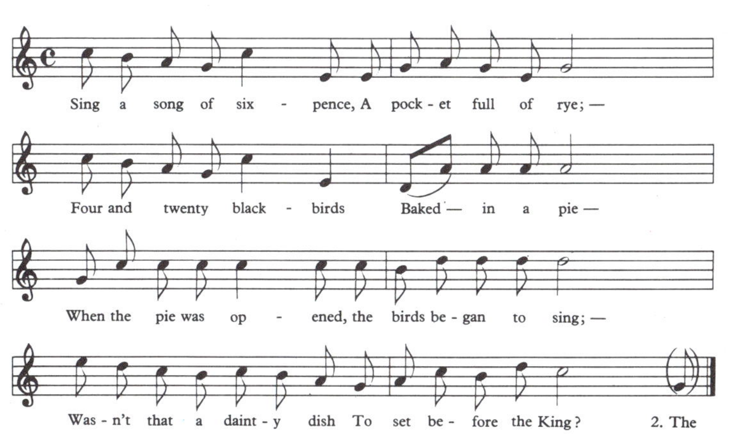
Sing a song of six - pence, A pock - et full of rye; —
Four and twenty black - birds Baked — in a pie —
When the pie was op - ened, the birds be - gan to sing; —
Was - n't that a daint - y dish To set be - fore the King? 2. The

The King was in his counting house,
Counting out his money;

The queen was in the parlour,
Eating bread and honey.

The maid was in the garden,
Hanging out the clothes,

When down came a blackbird
And pecked off her nose.

## *Do, do, pity my case*

Do, do, pity my case,
In some lady's garden;
My clothes to wash when I get home,
In some lady's garden.

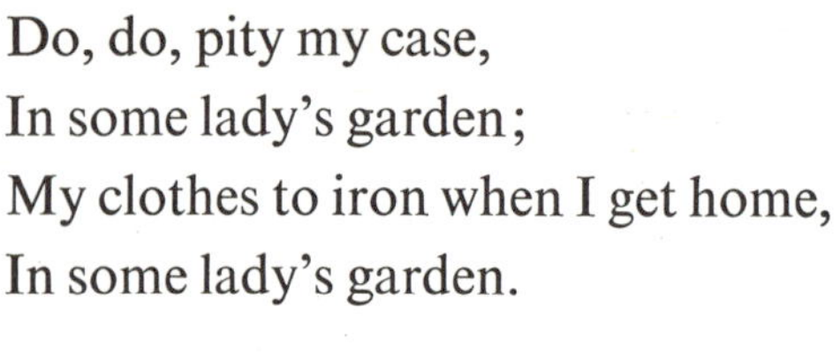

Do, do, pity my case,
In some lady's garden;
My clothes to iron when I get home,
In some lady's garden.

*The principal line in each verse should be mimed—washing clothes, ironing clothes, etc.*

Do, do, pity my case,
In some lady's garden;
My floors to scrub when I get home,
In some lady's garden.

Do, do, pity my case,
In some lady's garden;
My bread to bake when I get home,
In some lady's garden.

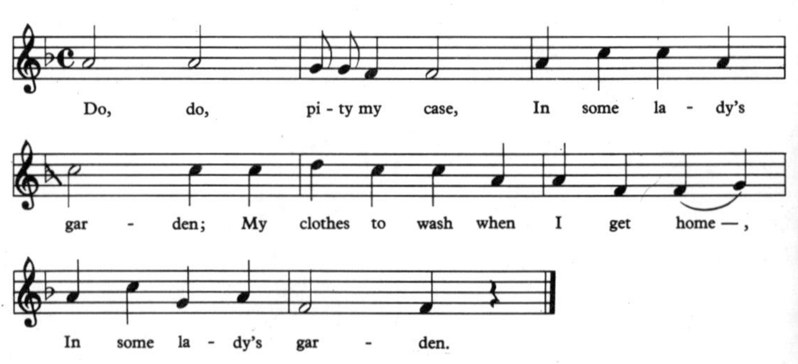

## *I had a little nut-tree*

I had a little nut-tree,
Nothing would it bear
But a silver nutmeg
And a golden pear;
The King of Spain's daughter
Came to visit me,
And all for the sake of my little nut-tree.
I skipped over water,
I danced over sea,
And all the birds in the air couldn't catch me.

*The child stands with arms wide (tree), circles an O in the air, then holds hands palms upward (holding nutmeg and pear). Hand to chest (visit of king's daughter), then tree again. Skipping, twirling, and arms waving (birds flying).*

# *When I was a shoemaker*

When I was a shoemaker,
And a shoemaker was I,
A-this-a-way, and a-this-a-way,
And a-this-a-way went I.

When I was a gentleman,
And a gentleman was I,
A-this-a-way, and a-this-a-way,
And a-this-a-way went I.

When I was a *lady*, etc.

When I was a *hairdresser*, etc.

*The children mime the action of the character.*

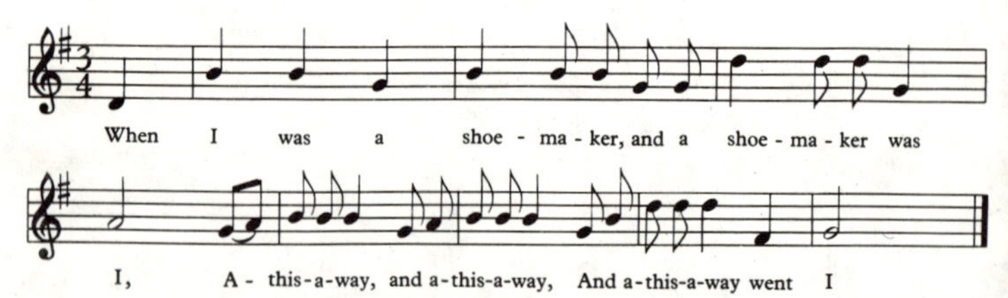

# *Soldier, soldier, won't you marry me*

'Soldier, soldier, won't you marry me,
With your musket, fife and drum?'
'Oh no, sweet maid, I cannot marry you,
For I have no hat to put on.'

*A boy and girl can mime the actions to these verses.*
*Girl stands with hands pointing to herself, boy shakes one hand from side to side and points to his head with the other.*
*Girl walks away and lifts lid of chest, brings out hat and gives it to boy who puts it on, etc.*

So off she went to her grandfather's chest,
And she brought him a hat of the very, very best,
And she brought him a hat of the very, very best,
And the soldier put it on!

'Soldier, soldier, won't you marry me,
With your musket, fife and drum?'
'Oh no, sweet maid, I cannot marry you,
For I have no coat to put on.'

So off she went to her grandfather's chest,
And she brought him a coat of the very, very best,
And she brought him a coat of the very, very best,
And the soldier put it on!

‘Soldier, soldier, won’t you marry me,
With your musket, fife and drum?’
‘Oh no, sweet maid, I cannot marry you,
For I have no boots to put on.’

So off she went to her grandfather’s chest,
And she brought him some boots
of the very, very best,
And she brought him some boots
of the very, very best,
And the soldier put them on!

‘Soldier, soldier, won’t you marry me,
With your musket, fife and drum?’
‘Oh no, sweet maid, I cannot marry you,
For I have a wife of my own!’

## *This is the way the ladies ride*

This is the way the ladies ride,
Nim, nim, nim, nim.
This is the way the gentlemen ride,
Trim, trim, trim, trim.
This is the way the farmers ride,
Trot, trot, trot, trot.
This is the way the huntsmen ride,
A-gallop, a-gallop, a-gallop, a-gallop.
This is the way the ploughboys ride,
Hobble-dy-gee, hobble-dy-gee, hobble-dy-gee.

*The children mime the different styles of riding mentioned.*

This is the way the la - dies ride, Nim, nim, nim, nim. This is the way the

gentlemen ride, Trim, trim, trim, trim. This is the way the farm - ers ride,

Trot, trot, trot, trot. This is the way the huntsmen ride, A- gal-lop, a-gal-lop, a -

gal - lop, a - gal - lop. This is the way the plough - boys ride Hob - ble - dy -

gee, hob - ble - dy - gee, hob - ble - dy - gee.

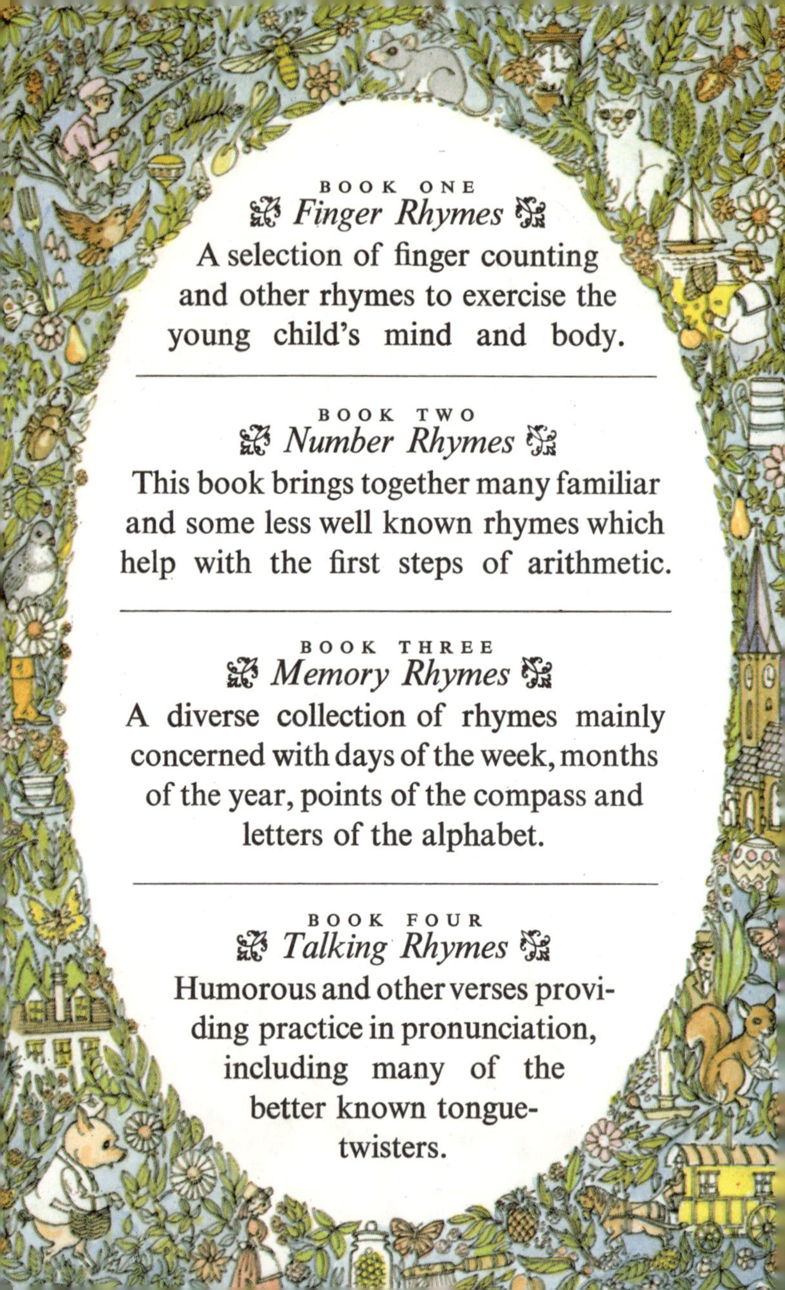

BOOK ONE

*Finger Rhymes*

A selection of finger counting and other rhymes to exercise the young child's mind and body.

---

BOOK TWO

*Number Rhymes*

This book brings together many familiar and some less well known rhymes which help with the first steps of arithmetic.

---

BOOK THREE

*Memory Rhymes*

A diverse collection of rhymes mainly concerned with days of the week, months of the year, points of the compass and letters of the alphabet.

---

BOOK FOUR

*Talking Rhymes*

Humorous and other verses providing practice in pronunciation, including many of the better known tongue-twisters.